ZOMBIE CREATURES

EMILY SCHLESINGER

red rhino b☉☉ks®

NONFICTION

SADDLEBACK
EDUCATIONAL PUBLISHING
www.sdlback.com

Photo credits: page 20/21: Papilio/Alamy Stock Photo; page 32/33: Natural Visions/Alamy Stock Photo; page 34: Scott Camazine/Alamy Stock Photo

ISBN: 978-1-68021-074-3
eBook: 978-1-63078-912-1

Printed in Malaysia

25 24 23 22 21   2 3 4 5 6

TABLE OF CONTENTS

Chapter 1
ZOMBIE COCKROACH

Green wings flash.

The jewel wasp waits.

Her next victim is near.

She is no match for its size.

But that does not matter.

She will take over its mind.

The *roach* is fast.

But the wasp is faster.

Poison is her plan.

She zaps the roach's legs.

They freeze.

The roach stops cold.

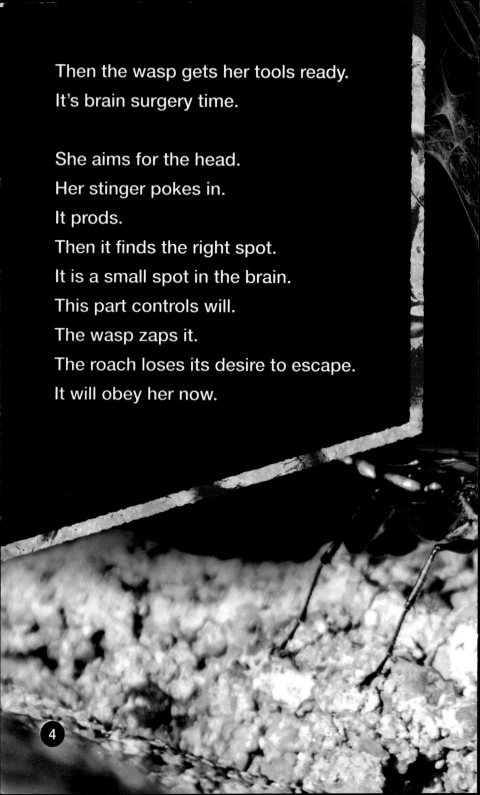

Then the wasp gets her tools ready.
It's brain surgery time.

She aims for the head.
Her stinger pokes in.
It prods.
Then it finds the right spot.
It is a small spot in the brain.
This part controls will.
The wasp zaps it.
The roach loses its desire to escape.
It will obey her now.

6

She takes a sip of its blood.
Then she grabs its antenna.
It makes a good leash.
She pulls.
The roach follows.
It trails her like a dog.
The wasp is its master.

They make a strange sight.
One holds a leash.
The other has a blank stare.
Together they march.
They head down a hole.

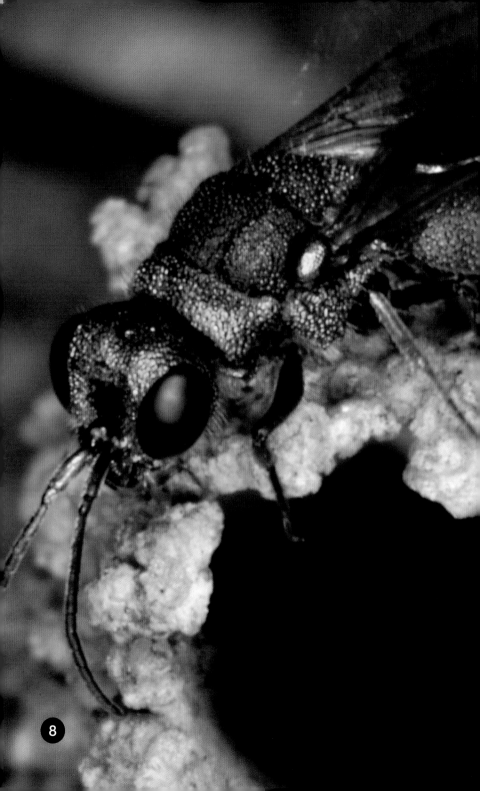

8

The roach has no clue.
But this is a tomb.
The wasp helps it climb in.
Then she piles small rocks around it.
Finally she lays an egg on its body.

Time goes by.
The egg hatches.
A *larva* is born.
It feeds on the roach.
The roach's shell is its cradle.
Soon there is a baby wasp.
It will find its own victim someday.
A *zombie* roach will raise its young.

This tale is creepy.
But it is not made up.
It is a true zombie story.
Nature is full of them.

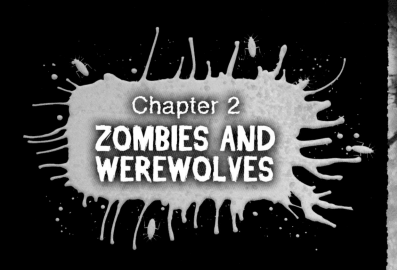

Chapter 2
ZOMBIES AND WEREWOLVES

Have you heard of a "Zombee"?
This is a zombie bee.

It leaves the hive at night.
The bee spins in circles.
It zigs and zags.
Then it dives.
Crash!

The bee is dazed.
It stumbles.
Then it explodes.
Flies pop out of the bee's body.
They were inside all along.

The flies hijacked the bee.
Then they drove it like a plane.
Crashing was their escape.

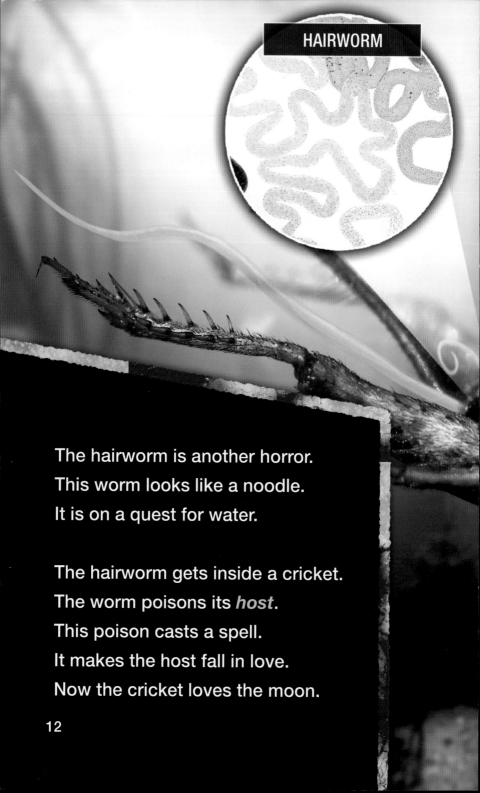

The hairworm is another horror.
This worm looks like a noodle.
It is on a quest for water.

The hairworm gets inside a cricket.
The worm poisons its *host*.
This poison casts a spell.
It makes the host fall in love.
Now the cricket loves the moon.

The cricket goes out at night.

There is the moon.

It reflects on a pond.

The cricket jumps in.

Then it drowns.

The hairworm crawls out.

Water is where the worm belongs.

CREEPY FACT

A mind control chemical
causes the cricket to move
toward light.

Chapter 3
THE SNAIL WITH CATERPILLAR EYES

These stories share one thing.

A creature must *survive*.

Some need a safe home.

Others must get to a place fast.

Using another creature helps.

A flatworm has a strange need.

It must get into a bird's belly.

That is where it can *reproduce*.

CREEPY FACT

This worm is called a
green-banded broodsac.
It has green stripes.

FLATWORM

The worm does something gross.

It crawls into a snail's eyes.

Now the eyes look plump and juicy.

They are full of worm.

The eyes grow and shrink as the worm moves.

They look like caterpillars.

Snails are shy.

They usually hide.

But this one does not.

You could say it turned over a new leaf.

Now it seeks open spaces.

A bird flies by.

It likes what it sees.

Juicy caterpillars wiggle.

It's like a fast food ad.

The bird can't say no.

It dives to its meal.

The worms win.

They made it to the bird.

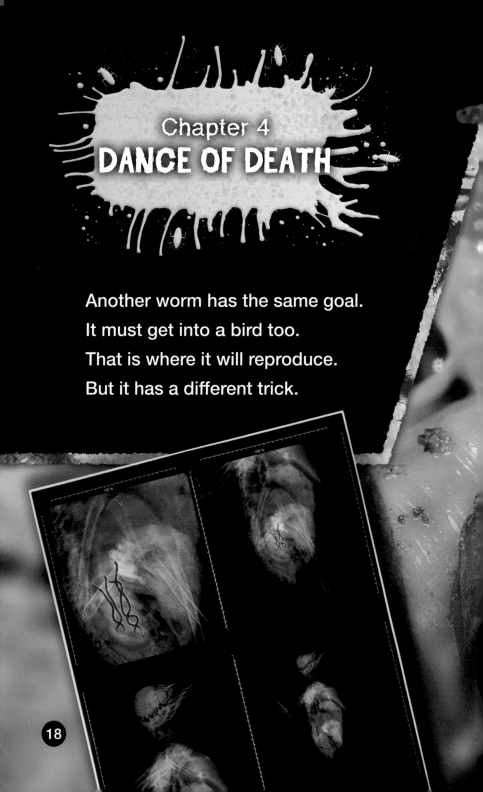

Chapter 4
DANCE OF DEATH

Another worm has the same goal.

It must get into a bird too.

That is where it will reproduce.

But it has a different trick.

CREEPY FACT

Gliding ants live in trees.
When they fall, they glide
gently to safety.

A gliding ant helps.

The ant eats the worm's eggs.

They hatch in its backside.

The ant's rear swells.

It looks like a ripe, red berry.

Worms take over the ant's mind.
Now the ant wants to dance.
It waves its rear in the air.
The ant shimmies and shuffles.
It can't stop.

A bird sees this.
What is going on?
It looks like a dancing berry.
That will make a tasty meal.
Gulp.

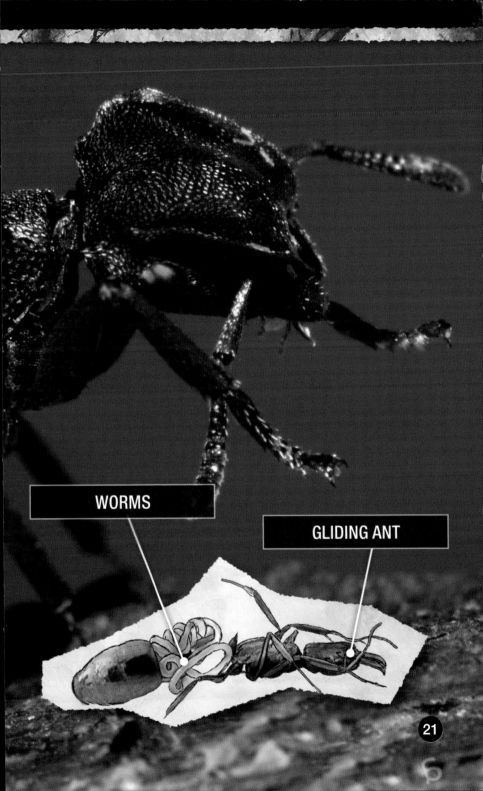

WORMS

GLIDING ANT

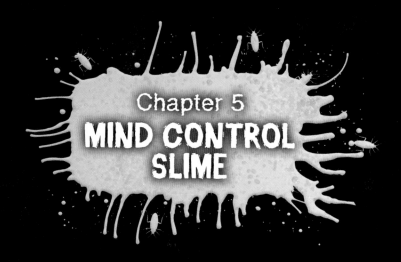

Chapter 5
MIND CONTROL SLIME

Nature's zombies are everywhere.

One creature is a host.

Another moves in.

This is an uninvited guest.

It takes control.

WORM EGGS

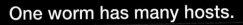

One worm has many hosts.

It moves from one to the next.

This is its *life cycle*.

First is a cow.

The worm goes into its *liver*.

It lays eggs there.

The cow poops.

Eggs come out too.

A snail is next.

It eats the eggs.

They hatch in the snail.

Mucus forms around each worm.

The snail coughs up this goo.

Slime balls fly.

They spread far.

An ant eats the slime.

The worm takes over its brain.

This ant gets an urge.

It wants to climb.

Up a blade of grass it goes.

It hangs out at the top.

The ant is not safe there at all.
It is like a meal on a stick.
A cow walks by.
It takes a bite.

What is next?
Ant and worm are swallowed.
Now the worm is back to square one.
It lays eggs in the cow's liver.
The cycle starts all over again.

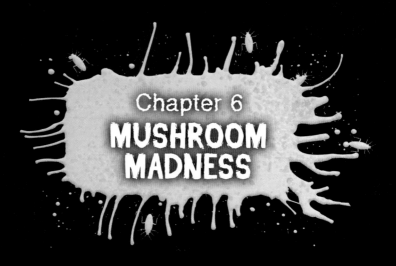

Chapter 6

MUSHROOM MADNESS

Parasites take over bodies.

They take over minds too.

But not all have minds of their own.

Some aren't even animals.

One is just a mushroom.

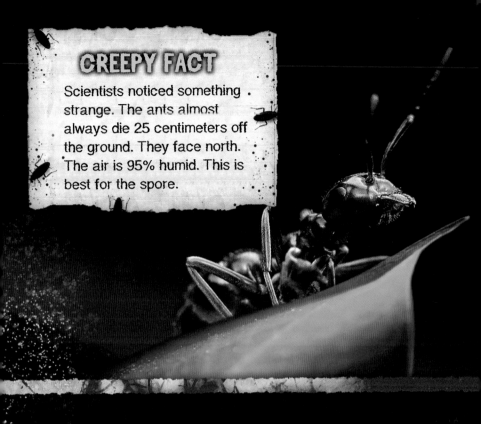

The mushroom drops *spores*.

An ant eats one.

The spores take over the ant's mind.

Now the ant has one goal.

It must climb to a certain leaf.

Only one will do.

It is almost a foot off the ground.

The ant's jaw chomps the leaf.

It is a death grip.

The ant dies on the spot.

27

Then something bursts out of the ant's head.
It is a mushroom.

The mushroom needed to get up there.

But it couldn't climb.

That is why it used the ant.

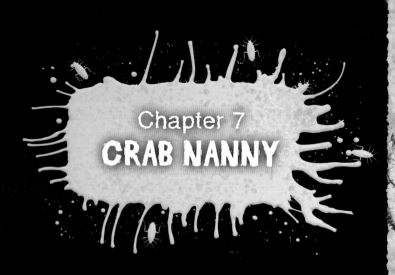

Chapter 7
CRAB NANNY

Parasites don't stop at mind control.
Some go further.
The *barnacle* is one.
This creature is tiny.
It lives in the sea.

The barnacle meets a crab.
Then it sheds its shell.
It crawls into the crab's claw.
What does the barnacle want?
Its young need care.
The crab will help.
It just doesn't know it yet.

CREEPY FACT

A barnacle parasite looks like an egg yolk stuck to the crab.

BARNACLE

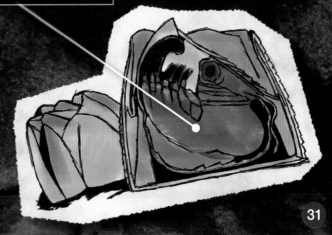

A female crab has a big belly.
She cares for babies there.
The barnacle is sneaky.
It puts its own babies in.
The crab has no idea.
She cares for them.
They are treated like her own.
She makes a great nanny.

But what if the crab is male?
That is a problem.
Or is it?
The barnacle has a simple fix.
It turns him into a female.

Chemicals do it.
A few changes are made.
The claws shrink.
A new belly is added.
It is a female belly.
Now the male is a mom.

Chapter 8
HOME HELP

Spiders have a skill.

Their webs turn heads.

Silk patterns take over the sky.

The webs are strong and light.

Spiders are true artists.

Most creatures can't do this.

But what if they got a spider to help?

One wasp does.

It lays an egg on a spider.

A larva hatches.

Then it squirts the spider with a *drug*.

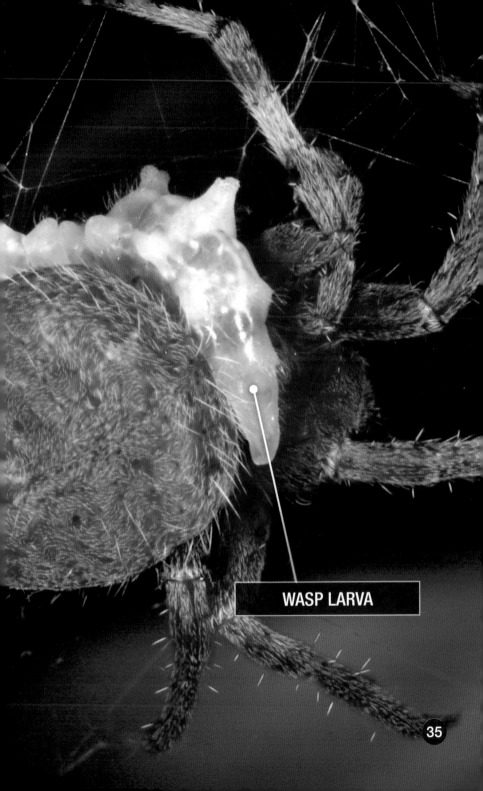

WASP LARVA

The spider is brainwashed.

It doesn't build its own web anymore.

Now it builds one for the larva.

This web is special.

The shape is a witch's broom.

It is not like anything the spider ever built.

And it's just what the larva needs.

The web makes the perfect hammock.

The larva moves to its new home.

How does it thank the spider?

It turns into a wasp and eats the spider.

CREEPY FACT

Scientists tested the new web.
It was 2.7 times stronger than
the normal web.

LARVA'S COCOON

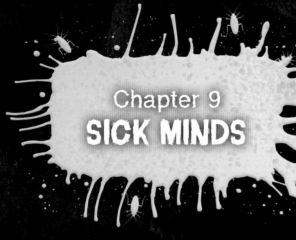

Chapter 9
SICK MINDS

Germs make us sick.
A *virus* is one.
It can cause a cold or *flu*.

Toxo is another.
This virus lives in a rat's brain.
But that is not its last home.
It must get into a cat.
That is the only place it can reproduce.

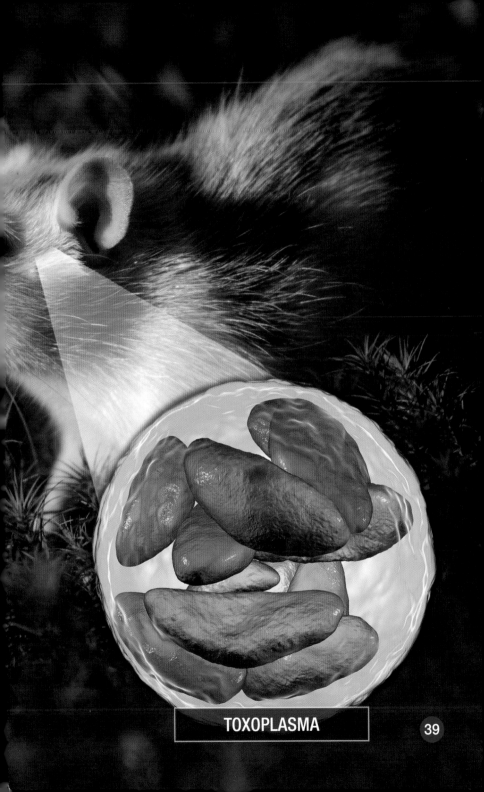

TOXOPLASMA

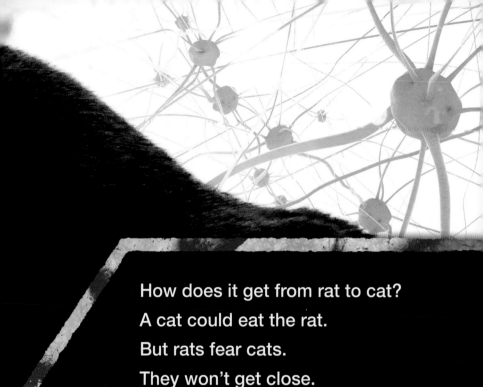

How does it get from rat to cat?
A cat could eat the rat.
But rats fear cats.
They won't get close.

Toxo changes this.
Its power is strong.
It takes away a rat's fear.
Now the rat hangs out near cats.
It likes the smell of cat urine.

You can guess what is next.
The rat gets eaten.
This is great for the toxo.
Life goes on in its new host.

A germ changed the rat's mind.
Could it change yours too?

Picture this.
You get the flu.
It makes you feel like a zombie.
You are not really one.
Or are you?

A study asked this question.
One group got a shot.
It had the flu in it.
One group did not.

CREEPY FACT

Up to half of humans have
toxo. Some think it makes
us cat lovers. But there is
no proof.

The first group acted different.

People grew more *social*.

Why would this be?

Think about it.

You go to see friends.

This spreads germs.

More pals mean more hosts for the virus.

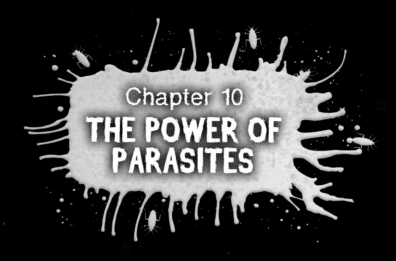

Chapter 10
THE POWER OF PARASITES

Parasites have power.

It makes us wonder.

How did they get so smart?

But they are not smart at all.

Their power comes from chance.

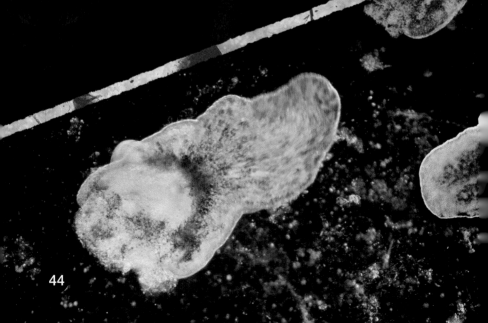

A creature has *offspring*.

It may have many.

Each is born with its own skills.

Some help it survive.

Others do not.

It's a roll of the dice.

Here are two viruses.

Which will *thrive*?

You make a guess.

VIRUS 1

1	Causes a caterpillar to eat a lot
2	Makes the caterpillar climb a tree
3	Explodes the caterpillar

VIRUS 2

1	Causes a caterpillar to eat a lot
2	Explodes the caterpillar

The answer is the first.

It makes its host climb a tree.

That is very useful.

The virus spreads farther that way.

It gets on leaves.

More creatures eat the virus.

Its numbers grow.

Nature is always changing.
Creatures *adapt*.
Babies are born with new skills.
They find new ways to survive.

New parasites will join us.
Their zombies will roam.
These stories will shock us.
The show will go on.

49

GLOSSARY

adapt: to change to fit better into an environment

barnacle: a small ocean animal with a shell

drug: a chemical that changes the body

flu: a virus that spreads from person to person

germ: a tiny organism or part of one that causes illness

host: an animal or plant with another organism living in or on it

larva: a young insect or other creature that is not yet an adult

life cycle: steps in an organism's life including birth, reproduction, and death

liver: an organ that helps clean the blood

mucus: a slimy substance produced by the nose or lungs

offspring: children or copies of an organism

parasite: an organism that lives in or on another organism

reproduce: to produce children or copies of an organism

roach: an insect with long legs, a shell, wings, and antennae

social: spending time in groups

spore: a cell that allows fungi and some plants to reproduce

survive: to stay alive in a difficult environment

thrive: to improve or be successful

virus: a substance that takes over an organism's cells and makes it sick

zombie: a creature that moves but no longer controls its own thoughts and actions

MILITARY DOGS

Chapter 4
A DOG'S NOSE

Think about your nose.
What if it was 100 times stronger?
A dog would still have a better nose.
It can smell 100,000 times better.

Here is an example.
Take a drop of sweat.
Spread it over a whole city.
A dog would notice it.

Dogs can pick apart smells too.
Picture a birthday party.
You smell a cake.
What does a dog smell?
It smells flour, eggs, and sugar.
Each part stands out.
Humans do not have this skill.

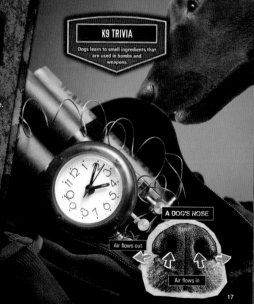

K9 TRIVIA
Dogs learn to smell ingredients that are used in bombs and weapons.

A DOG'S NOSE
Air flows out
Air flows in

Chapter 5
SCOUTING

The ability to smell is important in war.
A bomb may be near.
Or it could be a land *mine*.
Troops have no idea where.
But a dog can smell it.

Sniffing out threats is called scouting.
This is a dog's biggest strength.
It saves lives.

Cali was a scout.
She worked in the Army.
Her job was to sniff.
She found traps and mines.
Snipers could be around too.

Chris is a handler.
His dog is Kira.
The two were sent to Afghanistan.
They helped a special ops team.
Kira found *IEDs*.
These are a type of bomb.
"I take pride," Chris said.
"While Kira and I were out working, my guys did not get blown up."

The two took care of each other.
Chris would scratch her belly.
He rubbed her foot pads.
Chis explained why.
"She was out there making sure we were safe.
It wasn't much in return for what she did."

red rhino b👓👓ks®

NONFICTION

BIOWEAPONS

LESLIE RUTKIN

CANNIBAL ANIMALS

JOHN PERRITANO

CLONING

SUSAN HENNEBERG

AREA 51

COMET CATCHER

JOHN PERRITANO

DRONES
SUSAN HENNEBERG

FAULT LINES

JOHN PERRITANO

GNARLY
SPORTS INJURIES

JOHN PERRITANO

GREAT SPIES of the WORLD

JOHN PERRITANO

HACKED

M.G. HIGGINS

LITTLE ROCK NINE

JOHN PERRITANO

MEDAL OF HONOR

JOHN PERRITANO

MILITARY DOGS

EMILY SCHLESINGER

MONSTERS OF THE DEEP

JOHN PERRITANO

MONSTERS of Land

JOHN PERRITANO

MYSTERIOUS OBJECTS

EMILY SCHLESINGER

RACETRACKS

EMILY SCHLESINGER

The SCIENCE of MOVIES

JOHN PERRITANO

SEVEN WONDERS of ANCIENT WORLD

ARIANNE MCHUGH

3D PRINTING

JOHN PERRITANO

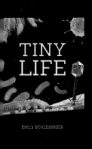

TINY LIFE

EMILY SCHLESINGER

TUSKEGEE AIRMEN

JOHN PERRITANO

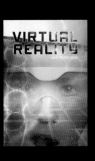

VIRTUAL REALITY

WILD WEATHER

JOHN PERRITANO

Witchcraft

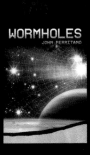

WORMHOLES

JOHN PERRITANO

ZOMBIE CREATURES

EMILY SCHLESINGER

WWW.REDRHINOBOOKS.COM

MORE TITLES COMING SOON